THE
TRANSFORMATIONAL
LENS

INDIA · SINGAPORE · MALAYSIA

Notion Press

No. 8, 3rd Cross Street,
CIT Colony, Mylapore,
Chennai, Tamil Nadu – 600 004

First Published by Notion Press 2020
Copyright © Yugandhar Penubolu 2020
All Rights Reserved.

ISBN 978-1-64951-864-4

THE
TRANSFORMATIONAL
LENS

Insights into people and performance management

A guide to enhance employee experience, capability, and growth

Yugandhar Penubolu

INDIA · SINGAPORE · MALAYSIA

INDICACADEMY

Indic Pledge

- *I celebrate our civilisational identity, continuity & legacy in thought, word and deed.*

- *I believe our indigenous thought has solutions for the global challenges of health, happiness, peace and sustainability.*

- *I shall seek to preserve, protect and promote this heritage and in doing so,*
    - *discover, nurture and harness my potential,*
    - *connect, cooperate and collaborate with fellow seekers,*
    - *advance diversity and inclusivity in the society.*

About Indic Academy

Indic Academy is a non-traditional 'university' for traditional knowledge. We seek to bring about a global renaissance based on Indic civilizational and indigenous thought. We are pursuing a multidimensional strategy across time, space and cause by establishing centers of excellence, transforming intellectuals and building an ecosystem.

Indic Academy is pleased to support this book.

To Diya, Tina
and
My Parents

Contents

Why I Wrote This Book!

I started writing this book with the experience of having been in the corporate world for over twenty years and the inspiration I gathered from a few people who had a profound influence on the way I practised management and leadership.

Over the years, I encountered various complex and tough situations but always rode the wave with my surf up. These exciting and eventful rides and experiences led to my realisation of the need to discover smarter and sustainable ways of managing people and processes in organisations. I learnt that the organisation's capability can be enhanced through empowerment, superior employee experience and higher learning quotient. I also learnt that a culture of embracing newness and change leads to successful transformations.

To enable this, leaders should focus on facilitating and providing actionable insights to their employees.

I wanted to share my version of how so many diverse opportunities are accessible through employees and can help both them and the organisations.

There are also a lot of concepts and theories which can be adopted into business and people processes. This can be done swiftly using technology in order to enhance the scope of development, output and effectiveness even while teams are working remotely.

And that's why this book happened; along with another leap in my graph – the beginning of my entrepreneurial journey – Winzard, a people performance platform providing solutions to leaders and employees for improving capability and achievement.

Credits

- My wonderful family who always believed in me and provided me the cushion to take the leap of faith each time!

- Great friends who encouraged me and gave me advice very often.

- Anand Joseph who helped write this book.

- Katyayani Ganti who helped edit this book.

- Lakshmi and notion team who helped in the publishing process.

- A week well spent discovering myself and the essentials of leadership with Prof. Daniel M. Cable and Prof. Herminia Ibarra at London Business School, from which I emerged feeling more alive at work and realised truly that what got me here wouldn't get me there!

- Experiencing turbulent yet exciting years of learning through the prime credit crisis and economic downturn, during which I worked as Vice President with Barclays Bank PLC.

- Some valuable years spent in a leadership role with Atria Convergence Technologies Limited experiencing the accompanying leadership challenges, understanding customer behaviour, loyalty and market dynamics.

- Enriching interactions with entrepreneurs over the past year, actively listening to the exciting growth stories and challenges that they face.

- Unprecedented COVID-19 times calling for resilience as well as transformation in the manner in which businesses are managed.

- Great bosses during my stints with GE, Standard Chartered, Barclays and ACT.

- Readers such as yourself, who encourage people like me to write and share our learnings, experiences and thoughts.

Introduction

"The spirit of an intrapreneur shows us that infinite opportunities await our will to seek."

This people and performance management book showcases essential elements that are required for organisations to ably sustain themselves and grow further, realising the full possible potential.

I have two objectives: I aim to provide valuable insights to leaders and managers in building and managing people processes effectively. I also aim to enable leaders and supervisors with some of the guiding principles that can potentially enhance the mindset of employees and capability of the entire organisation.

After some research, I chose to focus more specifically on those aspects that many leaders and employees often tend to neglect and avoid practising at work.

Using real life corporate examples, I want to stir up concepts pertaining to the organisational culture, its transformation, influencing teams and improving workplace synergies. This will help readers relate with these concepts and make use of relevant insights at work.

SECTION 1

Building Blocks

*N*oah, the Senior Vice President of a Non-Banking Finance Company, has been successfully managing loan sales of the organisation since its inception 6 years ago. This 750-member company which is managed by a highly experienced operations team has been growing at a steady pace.

The company recently started operations in 7 new cities and hired a hundred employees; those working for the company had never seen such a sudden influx of people. There were many ends to be fixed like ensuring that people got inducted into the organisation well, arranging the new workspaces and so on. Added to this, two larger challenges were at their doorstep – the Finance Minister introduced new lending regulations applicable to NBFCs, which needed to be complied with, and the bank lending rate also started to surge.

Noah and his peers found so many new developments overwhelming and were on firefight mode. They focussed on issues needing immediate attention such as remotely managing the new team members, setting up processes in new locations, as well as revising financial projections owing to changes in interest rates.

Noah had micro-managed operations to a large extent in the initial years, and he felt uncomfortable to rely heavily on inputs from the newer location managers. Now that the organisation had grown into a much larger one with more people and higher complexity, he realised the immediate need for him to empower key members and to effectively use the talent of the organisation. This would help him free most of his time spent on operations to concentrate on building networks and organisational transformation.

Organisation's Challenges and Expectations

The above example of Noah helps us understand that organisations deal with complex and diverse issues simultaneously. And leaders tend to find themselves firefighting to meet process and regulatory adherence apart from catering to staff and client expectations.

Leaders like Noah, who had dealt with and mentored teams personally while the organisation was smaller, may start to perceive people's engagement and capability with dated and limited interactions, leading to a trust deficit and demotivation.

The same leader, who has so far successfully managed the company, is now faced with handling new and tough scenarios, which he may not know how to manage.

Some of the challenges are:

- Low accountability
- Managing transformation
- Operations scalability
- Attrition management

The question in such a scenario is this: How could the leader channelise efforts in building a sustainable and fit organisation which is capable of progression in this ever-changing business environment?

Noah and the other leadership team members need to focus on building the right foundation through cohesive teams which are empowered and accountable in the organisation. Defining and communicating the right values, behaviours, vision, and purpose will serve as direction and a reference for all interpersonal dealings in the organisation.

[1]Culture represents the collective values, beliefs and principles of organisational members and is heavily weighted towards the head of the organisation and its leadership team. It is said to have the highest influence on the way people interact, the context within which knowledge is created, the resistance they will have towards certain changes, and ultimately the way they share knowledge.

This culture, however, keeps transforming. The aim is that the transformation helps the organisation progress into an inclusive one where there is visible commitment, healthy curiosity and effective collaboration. An organisation where employees practice these would find it easier to prioritise, organise and work cohesively in teams to provide clients with great products and service.

What Employees Seek

It is a known and accepted fact that organisations are made of employees whose basic expectations are:

- Money
- Respect

Their aspirations within the organisation revolve around:

- Work-life balance
- Growth (learning and career)

Most employees tend to go through phases of emotional stress and anxiety if they feel that any of the above four aspects are unsatisfactory or unmet.

On the contrary, it is seen that active engagement of an employee grows considerably if these above four elements are met.

With active employee engagement, employees would feel a higher sense of belonging followed by higher accountability. So, if leaders understood their employees well, the organisation would benefit greatly. They would also realise that highly engaged employees would strive to deliver great customer experience.

[2]*"All employees have an innate desire to contribute to something bigger than themselves."*

– Jag Randhawa

The Bridge between Seeking and Accountability

[3]Prof Dan Cable in his book *Alive At Work* explains that organisations control employees due to the fear of not meeting the expectations of their clients and stakeholders. This control limits the employees' ability to perform and manage only the tasks set out for them.

The fear that deviation from task description might result in negative consequences, would stall innovation and creativity. This confinement also makes the job feel mundane, limiting the seeking quotient for purpose and excellence. Yet, employees instinctively seek to discover and explore.

So, while an environment of accountability without seeking calls for low creativity, a balance between the seeking mindset of employees and accountability could set a path that enables change and leverages strengths for growth.

Leaders could balance the two by setting direction/ expectation/goals and empower employees with processes and platforms that help employees with planning their work, sharing learnings and ideation. This culture alone has the potential to improve ownership and engagement at the workplace.

Those who work towards enhancement of capability would be more resilient and confident in managing themselves, their teams and planning growth.

For enhancement of capability, improvement of four key capacities will help.

[4]Robert Glazer, in his book *Elevate*, explains that building Spiritual, Intellectual, Physical and Emotional capacities will aid in success while reducing the struggle during difficult situations.

Let us understand how to enhance these four capacities in this context:

Spiritual Capacity: What do I need? Why do I need it? What is the purpose? What are my core values? These need to be defined, and then aligned to goals.

Physical Capacity: Build this capacity by being conscious of health, managing stress and embracing competition.

Emotional Capacity: Build this capacity by seeking elevating relationships, trying the unfamiliar and practising resilience.

Intellectual Capacity: This capacity can be built by adopting a growth mindset, finding mentors, creating a habit of routines and expanding your network.

We will now delve into certain chapters which will cover aspects that form the foundation and growth drivers of the organisation.

ONE

EMPLOYEE EXPERIENCE AND SAFETY

Within an organisation, focusing on employee experience creates a work environment that inspires employees. Organisations invest in providing a conducive environment for employees to have least distraction and feel inspired to own their work and seek purpose.

Employee engagement is one of the most important growth drivers of an organisation, and it is a direct outcome of employee experience.

Employees have experiences that impact their engagement at work. A particular individual can have varied engagement levels at different time frames due to their personal perception, expectations and experience.

Hierarchy does not have a bearing on their engagement – it is not necessary that juniors are less engaged than their seniors. It has been noticed in many engagement surveys that quite a few organisations found lower engagement levels at middle and senior management levels than that of juniors. This shows that one must not assume that the focus must be on improving the engagement levels of lower grades or front-end staff.

Broadly, employees can be classified into 4 groups:

1. Actively engaged: Employees who are motivated, accountable and also believe that organisation is poised to succeed. Also, happy with their work and workplace.

2. Moderately engaged: Those who are reasonably engaged barring few factors that are keeping them from active engagement.

3. Disengaged: Those employees who do not associate themselves with outcomes. They are not happy at work but come to work to perform their job for lack of a better alternative or lack of ambition.

4. Cynical: Those who dislike the organisation and can potentially have a negative influence on their colleagues at the workplace.

It is obvious that organisations with more actively engaged employees have higher chances of succeeding.

Also, employees do not remain in the same engagement category at all times – employees often shift amongst the first three groups at different time frames.

However, any organisation with a high (>25%) count of employees in the disengaged and cynical group surely needs to review/alter its manner of functioning.

In an organisation, it was noticed that a senior employee came to the workplace only to complete the tasks at hand and leave. The person was satisfied with mediocre output and never seemed to be interested in planning for operational improvements. He also didn't take active interest in meetings and seemed clearly disengaged.

Some of the directly relatable questions that might be raised in this context are:

- What is causing this disengagement?
- How can the engagement quotient be improved?

Engagement is largely influenced by the culture of the organisation and daily work experience. The key influencing factors are leadership, superiors, job role, psychological and physical well-being, work ethics, and performance management systems impacting their income or career. It is important to understand which of these factors are adversely impacting engagement, and which are the driving factors of active engagement. Organisations need to also understand if certain work policies or methods are the source of disengagement.

For understanding employee engagement, an employee engagement survey can be conducted. Apart from being curated well, the survey should also give insights on blind spots and engagement levels.

While doing a deep dive using the insights from the survey results, it is important to identify the source of the issue. Is it an overall culture problem that stems from the leadership where there is a general feeling of office politics throughout the organisation? It could be a work process problem that needs to be addressed, like improper training. It could be limited to a particular department within the company, where a particular manager ignores work-life balance. Sometimes particular age groups don't feel part of the company, or there is harassment based on gender at a particular location. So, it is important that the engagement survey provides these insights while being able to filter results based on various groups such as units, gender, age, grade, location, apart from any other category that is important to an organisation.

Once the problem areas have been identified, the next step is to devise a concrete plan of action.

Creating accountability and assigning action plans for implementation of measures would ensure that focus on the plan to improve employee engagement is not lost.

The Leadership team should also convey key findings to all employees. By showcasing the action plans, employees understand the seriousness with which the organisation is focusing on people issues, employee happiness and well-being.

Since insights are inputs on key areas of improvement, leaders should take these insights as opportunities to improve. No team with low engagement should be blamed or ridiculed, instead, they are to be understood and mentored to maintain an environment of positivity and improvement.

An unsafe environment is a breeding ground for low productivity, disengagement, and cynicism.

Over time, employees would actively look to find more suitable workplaces that may appear safe.

An important factor that influences employee experience is workplace safety, and the next few pages explain some important aspects pertaining to it and what can be done to make employees feel safe at work.

Employees could feel unsafe due to discrimination, unsafe business practices, favouritism, grudges, poor infrastructure, cultural issues, supervisor behaviour, policies, harassment apart from so many others.

Workplace safety can be broadly classified into:

- Physical safety
- Psychological safety
- Social safety
- Professional safety

Physical well-being and safety can be improved by:

- Providing safe workplace infrastructure and equipment
- Awareness with regards to the risks involved
- Communicating procedures regularly
- Establishing a robust monitoring system
- Gathering information periodically to understand possible areas of concern
- Ensuring that best practices are followed to avoid accidents

However, even if procedures and monitoring systems for aspects such as fire and security, etc. are put in place by the organisation, it is imperative that employees consider safety as the most important aspect, and not allow any lax on the established precautions.

Psychological safety can only be embedded through a major cultural focus involving the whole organisation.

[5]A 2016 *New York Times* article shared findings of a research involving 180 Google teams that studied the contributing factors that made the best teams. And, researchers found that the most important characteristic of a good team was psychological safety.

*Psychological Danger & Psychological Safety

(Exhibit 1)   (Exhibit 2)

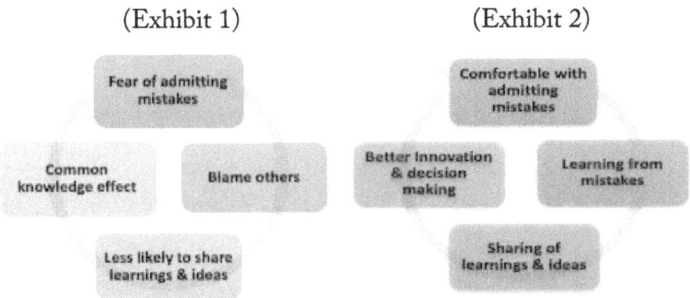

*https://www.weforum.org/agenda/2016/04/team-psychological-danger-work-performance/

At times, managers think that fear is a key tool to push employees into having tasks accomplished. But as seen in Exhibit 1, fear of negative consequences leads to blaming others instead of admitting mistakes and learning from them. Fear often leads to disengagement towards outcome or adoption of unethical business practices.

In such an atmosphere, employees deeply fear being perceived as incompetent or labelled as unintelligent or being ridiculed. As seen in Exhibit 2, with a culture of sharing ideas and experiences, innovation and creativity are encouraged. This increases the probability of better output.

An environment with high accountability and low psychological safety creates anxiety. It potentially leads to the possibility of an untoward incident occurring or even high attrition. On the other hand, in a workspace with high accountability and psychological safety, one seeks and learns to deliver. For this culture of high psychological safety and accountability to be adopted by all, the leader needs to inculcate the belief that the organisation truly cares and believes in providing a safe workplace.

[6]*"Leadership is practiced not so much in words as in attitude and in actions."*

– Harold S. Geneen

In other words, the leader should walk the talk. They should:

- Be authentic
- Be humble
- Respect diversity
- Share personal learning moments
- Admit failure

This sets the tone for workplace interactions, and a similar behaviour would be adopted by the managers and supervisors.

Any occurrence of exploitation or harassment at the workplace is unmistakably a failure of Physical or Psychological safety. It is unfortunate that very often incidents are not even escalated or reported owing to the fear of the organisation's lack of empathy.

What is worse is that some leaders take pride in building a workaholic and stressful workplace; this is aided by zealous goals and ambitions. In the short run it may seem like aggressive goals are achieved, but more often than not, this kind of work culture leads to multiplied stress-levels and cynicism amongst the employees in the long run. Individuals suffer from burnout and disengagement which will lead to drop in productivity, toxic work culture or/and a high rate of attrition.

No matter how close the deadline or how ambitious the project, exploiting team members is not a healthy practice; unfortunately, this kind of work ethic is often misunderstood as simply demanding hard work.

Sexual harassment is a form of unsafe practice which in most cases is more psychological, but in a few cases could and has breached physical safety as well.

Zara, a tele-sales representative in AB Tech, approached Rakesh, a senior trainer in the company seeking advice in order to improve her call quality. A few days later, Rakesh offered her a lift in his car while she was walking home, which she accepted. While in the car, he started enquiring details about her personal life and made her uncomfortable. The same evening, he called on her phone asking her to join him on a date, which she declined. After that day, Zara started to avoid his persistent calls. She confided in her friend at work about this disturbing development of persistent calls from Rakesh, who thought it was right to escalate the matter to the unit manager.

Despite Zara's complaint, the unit manager did not take it seriously nor did he think it necessary to report the incident to HR.

It is important, and extremely so, for every organisation to reduce the probability of such incidents being neglected and reinforce the organisation's employee-caring ideology. Also, assure confidentiality and zero tolerance towards harassment.

In order to prevent the occurrence of sexual harassment instances, leaders should:

- Provide awareness and insights to the employees about sexual harassment, explain their right to a workplace free of harassment and report when anyone faces such a situation.

- Provide training to supervisors and managers about handling occurrences of sexual harassment, look for indications or early signs, and how to sensitively deal with complaints.

- Introduce and publish an Anti-Sexual Harassment policy amongst all the employees.

- Establish a PoSH (Prevention of Sexual Harassment) committee within the organisation, which manages prevention, prohibition, and redressal as per policy and the provisions of the law.

This kind of approach can be taken for other types of harassment as well.

It is to be noted that women are not the only ones who get sexually harassed. Though it doesn't occur as much, there are cases of women sexually harassing men at the workplace as well.

Social safety issues at workplaces range from ridiculing, segregation and alienation from the rest of the team, unjustified blame and being treated unfairly in general. Office politics plays a part as well.

Especially since emotional harassment has a very high occurrence rate and most often goes unnoticed, it is very important that the culture of the organisation is adapted to ensure this doesn't occur. Harassment is one of the biggest contributors to disengagement, low productivity and high rates of attrition.

Social safety can be improved by publishing guidelines, creating awareness and showcasing the probable impact pertaining to the following:

- Ensuring zero tolerance towards politics, power imbalance and bullying at the workplace
- Promoting an open and diverse culture and discouraging discrimination
- Having a positive and open communication climate and a defined system where employees

can speak up their opinions and concerns without fear of being ridiculed

Professional safety can be improved by leaders by showcasing rightful behaviour and with examples pertaining to:

- Ethics and moral standards expectation in policies and in practice
- Provision of reasonable job security and reducing anxiousness
- Approach of fairness in all processes
- Not demanding employees to do illegal work
- Maintenance of professionalism by encouraging an honest work environment and expecting highest integrity

Apart from the above, successful and competent leaders regularly assess progress and build a culture where unproductive work/practices/meetings are eliminated entirely providing employees with more time to spend on constructive tasks. This helps avoid working for long hours.

It is also imperative that both leaders and teams should hold themselves accountable for an effective workplace.

TWO

COHESIVE TEAMS

C ohesive teams have a higher probability of success.

Many leaders tend to presume cohesiveness within teams as a given and expect teams to dish out results together only to find out that their involvement is required.

Trust and respect are fundamental aspects that help spirited teams work together, making them formidable forces in the organisation. Such teams make the journey easier and its members work towards achievement with the spirit of togetherness. Members of a group or unit, when made to feel empowered, will challenge and inspire each other, manage vulnerabilities and face challenges better. But the quality of communication, or lack of it, can make or break the aspects mentioned above. And, the responsibility of quality communication amongst team members rests entirely with its leader – they are the ones who instil a culture in which uniqueness is encouraged, team stories are shared, efforts are recognised and achievements are appreciated.

At this point, it would seem imperative to mention that evaluation of the content is done before the leaders communicate and so they should always:

- Keep in mind the diversity and sensitivity of the groups.
- Recognise that the unique strengths of each member would partner the strengths of the others in the team, turning it into a formidable force that combines energy, ideation and agility.
- Celebrate their successes together knowing well that each member is unique, and each situation does not call for equal contribution.

While gaining the confidence of the group or pitching a point, it is recommended to plan in advance and be concise.

Many leaders follow the **PREP**[7] method –

- Make the **Point**
- Explain the **Reason**
- Give an **Example**
- Then conclude with the **Point**

A good leader must, at any cost, avoid labelling.

Instead of using words such as good, bad or excellent, the leader should speak in a manner in which it comes across to the employee that his/her work or strategy is being acknowledged and recognised. This kind of communication from the leader greatly influences the employee's mindset and encourages them to channelise effort towards improvising their methods further.

Great teams push each other to succeed; they work, resolve conflicts, support each other and celebrate success together. However, there could be situations when the employees face trust deficit and conflicts.

According to Prof. Frances Frei[8], there are 3 elements that greatly aid leaders and managers, in building trust:

- Authenticity
- Rigour for logic
- Empathy

If the employee sees any of the 3 elements missing, it would result in a case of trust deficit in the leadership.

Leadership plays its role in ensuring that teams become cohesive and not dysfunctional.

[9]Lencioni's pyramid of trust explains that absence of trust in the leader, manager or management leads to fear of conflicts, avoidance of accountability and disengagement with outcomes.

Exhibit 3 and 4 shown below explain the distinct behaviours of cohesive teams and dysfunctional teams.

Team Behaviours

Cohesive Team[10]	Dysfunctional team[11]
(Exhibit 3)	(Exhibit 4)

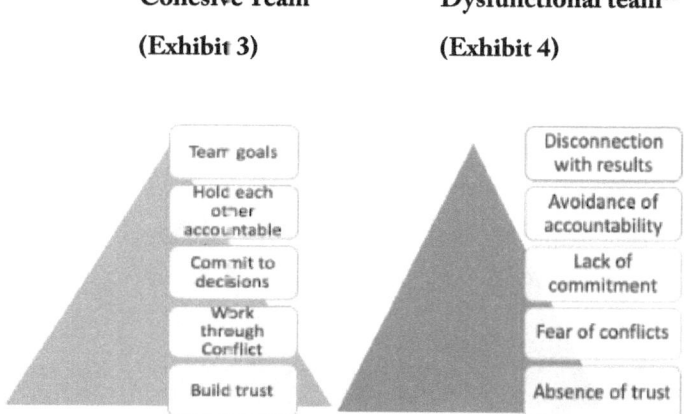

(Inspired by the Lencioni Model)

Exhibit 3 shows that five key behaviours define cohesive teams:

- Trust
- Work through conflicts
- Commitment
- Accountability
- Collective focus on results

It can be seen in Exhibit 4 that due to lack of trust, team members fear facing conflicts and avoid commitment since they may be criticised and blamed when mistakes happen. Lack of commitment leads to low accountability towards the goals or task. They tend to form this mindset of disconnection with the team and with the outcomes or results.

The leaders ensure teams are cohesive and don't become dysfunctional by playing their role.

- They play the role of collaborating teams towards collective outcomes by facilitating team goals.
- They confront difficult issues as a team and showcase being accountable.
- They force clarity in teams and encourage commitment to closure.
- They participate in healthy conflicts and views.
- They showcase their trust in the teams and members.

Leaders build cohesive teams by practising what they preach, encouraging teams, participating in healthy arguments, readying the team to embrace challenges, and reaching collective outcomes.

THREE

EMPOWERMENT THROUGH LEARNING AND INSIGHTS

[12]Bill Gates once said, "As we look ahead into the next century, leaders will be those who empower others."

A culture of learning and growth mindset in people processes has the potential to enhance the organisation's overall capability.

Employees have the innate potential to plan and own their work. In order to put that in practice, they need to feel empowered and have access to great insights.

Providing learning opportunities could be the best form of empowerment. This empowerment along with their combined potential could result in a better plan in order to build a wonderful enterprise.

For employees in many organisations, learning is a personal journey or is aided through 2 to 3 curated workshops each year conducted by the company depending on their function and level/grade. This needs to change!

Learning gives an advantage to the individual, and the knowledge acquired empowers the individual.

There is a successful example to be found in Satya Nadella, CEO of Microsoft. He focussed on transforming Microsoft's workforce culture from "Know it All" to "Learn it All" inspired by [13]Dr. Dweck's book on growth mindset.

Such leaders have explained and urged others to encourage and empower employees through learning.

However, the unfortunate reality is that some employees don't value learning, and some are not driven enough to learn. This could be because their initial experience may not have been interesting or fruitful, or they might be intimidated by books that run into hundreds of pages, or simply because they lack the drive to go through the effort of finding relevant content.

With an approach where the focus is on understanding information and concepts for learning and also teaching, the employees' interest could be triggered.

Again, merely triggering interest would not give results unless learning is put to action. Action using the input (learning) is what helps in delivering results. So, the application of learning is necessary, and employees should be encouraged to showcase and use learnings at work.

Yet, the question is whether the encouragement and understanding of concepts are leading to a culture of learning and growth mindset?

Tina worked for an Insurance firm, where their job involved having to do mandatory certifications that permit individuals to sell or underwrite insurance policies.

To Tina, learning in her organisation was limited to reading the circular of certification exercise. The firm too believed that the learning platform was created for people to read material that helped directly in their jobs. It was a one-way process where the material was loaded for reading, after which the employee took the test, and the resulting certification was showcased to the individual and HR.

While such a process adopted by the company was relevant and would aid employees to perform well at their jobs, wouldn't organisations ideally want employees to be creative, adaptive to change and also learn other aspects that could add value to both the individual and organisation beyond the current scope of job?

Could the organisation and employee cultivate learning as a choice, as an exciting opportunity to explore and enhance employee's capabilities for being future ready as well?

How could the organisation help the employees improve their eagerness and learning quotient?

As an individual, the one aspect that has fuelled my learning has been curiosity. When I read or see things, there is an inert sense of wanting to know how and why. And in this day and age, with information available at your fingertips, it's very easy to search for answers.

To develop a sense of curiosity, one needs to just keep asking questions of what, why and how. And learning will automatically stem from there. On the other hand, the organisation could post weekly Micro Learnings (which can be defined as posts that can be read in under 1 minute) to engage even the busiest employee owing to the short time it demands. Many employees would look forward to these posts, while assessing their relevance to their own work and life.

It is known that the higher the learning quotient of employees, the higher the organisation's capability.

Knowledge and clearly defined expectations reduce fear of unfamiliar territory or misconceived notions; and lower fear leads to trying and doing more.

To begin with, facilitating a well-equipped self-learning platform managed by the employees themselves could encourage the culture of seeking, after which the process of learning would naturally begin. The same platform could host the company-led training schedule, content and also the library of induction/white papers/reference work material, etc. for easy reference.

ENHANCEMENT OF LEARNING QUOTIENT

(Exhibit 5)

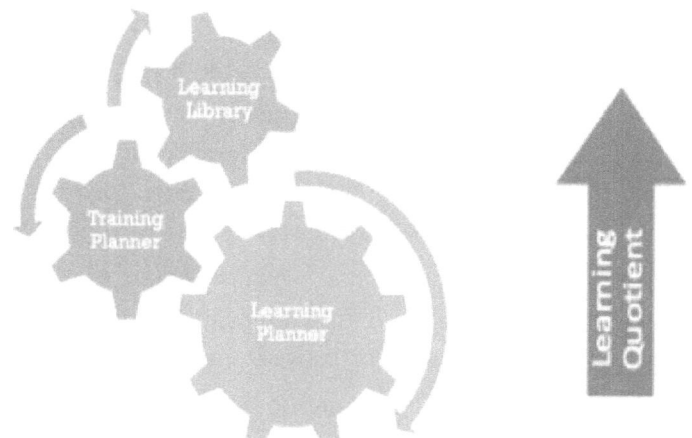

Such a platform could also motivate employees to share, showcase ideas or set personal learning goals and results.

With a growth mindset, the bigger the challenge, the more the probability the employee would stretch. [14]Dr. Dweck agrees that failures are painful, but they do not define you. It is a problem to be faced, to be dealt with and to learn from.

Equipped with a growth mindset, employees begin to:

- Embrace challenges
- Persist and discover that effort leads to growth
- Learn from mistakes and from success of others

[15]When a child solves a difficult and complex mathematical problem, the parent may praise the child by saying, "You are very smart." But, such praise would lead to a fixed mindset. Instead, if the parent compliments the child by saying, "I like the way you have applied your learning to solve this problem" or "I am happy to see how you used the right method and thought process to solve the problem," it would lead to developing a growth mindset in the child. Through this, the child would associate application of effort, strategy or learning to achieve rather than develop an exaggerated self-image. By developing such an image of one's self, and thereby a fixed mindset, the child may stop learning, avoid embracing challenges and credit the inherent smartness to any success achieved, not the effort put in to do so.

For every employee, the belief that they are in control of their own ability and can learn to improve is the key to success. Of course, hard work, effort, and persistence are all important, but nothing boosts confidence like having that underlying belief that s/he is in control of his/her own destiny.

The culture of sharing learnings and ideas would prove to be the source for innovation. A work culture which encourages employees to share learnings and ideas without the fear of committing mistakes can benefit the entire team, and the number of mistakes actually committed by the entire team would go down.

Those in the positions of supervisors and leaders have the biggest role to play in creating a work environment that facilitates enhancement of the learning quotient and encourages a growth mindset.

The expectation is that teams are actively engaged and accountable at work without the fear of failure.

What is the need to empower employees with actionable insights?

Every new limit tested or a new finishing line crossed inspires the human spirit with reinstated energy and resilience – like in sports or education, where records are broken time and again in various ways. Every record created stands like a factor that challenges successors to cross it.

Statistical data aids us in understanding the limiting factors, progression statistics, learnings, probabilities, but more importantly, it highlights the previous finishing line.

The Management uses such insights at every phase of the organisation's journey for decision making and to plan action. But, these insights could many a time be influenced or biased, and moreover, not derived from credible information. Any action taken based on such information could lead to serious people and process challenges, potentially denting the organisation's progress.

Every employee amply aided by actionable insights can take informed action or employ course- correction.

A holistic platform that could ideally analyse data, facilitate planning and help execution shall empower the employees with clear direction, aid in work planning, delegation, monitoring, and development.

Regular insights help the leadership to act on specific areas needing attention and also take informed action confidently based on various dimensions that impact progress.

However, these insights should not be limited to Management. The best empowerment that leaders could provide to their employees is to equip them with simple and sharp insights for self-introspection, progress on goals, career path, personal working style, challenges, latest market developments, trends, reference documents and development areas, etc.

Similarly, it is important not to undermine feedback which is a great insight in itself. So, feedback mechanisms could be built within the platform giving insights pertaining to employees, processes, management and customers.

Insights could bring about changes in perception, help in responsible communication and act as food for thought.

Showcasing relevant information to the employees also gives them an understanding of the organisation's journey and progress such as the plans, methods, options and external environment.

Equipped with common purpose, good employee experience and great insights, the organisation is poised with the right building blocks. What it now needs is to be agile in managing the changing business environment, innovate for growth and even lead in the market.

A RECAP OF THE KEY POINTS COVERED

- Defining vision, values and purpose
- Enhancement of capability
- Balancing accountability and seeking
- Employee Engagement – Insights and action planning
- Workplace safety concerns and its impact
- Cohesive and dysfunctional teams
- Enhancing the learning quotient
- Why holistic platforms for insights are needed!

KEY TAKE-AWAYS

ACTION PLANS

SECTION 2

Transformation

It is fascinating to note how varied methods are being used in similar businesses by different leaders.

While some organisations benefit from service or product superiority, some find that good networking proves to be an asset, and for others, marketing is the key element for success and so on.

There does not seem to be one definitive method, but the evolution of internal and external environments has forced organisations to change their methods. The skills and experience of the leaders play an important role in this as well. Thus, transformation seems to be decisive in order for an organisation to be relevant and competitive in this fast paced and evolving business environment.

There are numerous needs for transformation that demand focus, but a few fundamental ones will be stressed upon in the next few chapters:

- Transformational leadership
- Culture of adopting change as a growth driver
- Culture of Innovation

FOUR

TRANSFORMATIONAL LEADERSHIP

If the leader focuses on creating the foundation which provides well for transformation drivers like change, innovation and leadership, the organisation will evolve admirably, embracing external changes and building synergies to even lead the transformation in the market.

Since managing organisational transformation is critical, the need for transformational leaders arises. So, let's first delve upon the distinction between transactional and transformational leadership.

Generally, it is understood that transactional leadership[16] purely focuses on achieving the set goals and for this they:

- Direct employees to follow structures/checklists
- Use rewards and penalty as a driving force
- Are responsive
- Closely monitor the progress of employees

The shortcomings of this kind of leadership is mainly a reduced scope of ideation and innovation.

Transformational leadership[17]

(Exhibit 6)

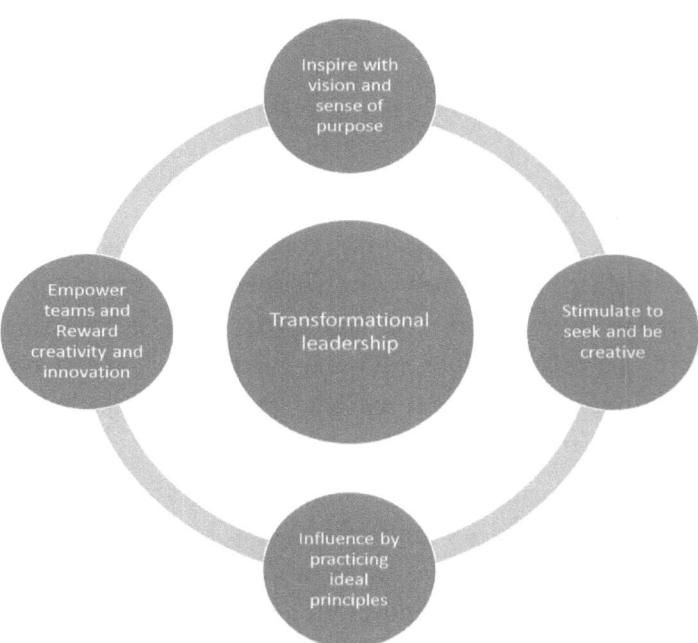

On the other hand, transformational leaders as seen in Exhibit 6:

- Proactively inspire teams with vision and by seeding a sense of purpose
- Practice what they preach and encourage team members to seek and be creative

- Mentor team members
- Reward ideation

Transformational leaders can be found at different levels of the hierarchy.

Another behavioural trait that is important and needs to be encouraged is taking note of internal as well as external events and challenges. Then, sparking the creativity in teams with inspiration and empowering them to come up with solutions to manage the transformation is needed.

Since transformation is understood to be a continuous evolution of processes, barring a few exceptions, the leaders should ensure internal processes of the organisation are designed to and subjected to:

- Review
- Learn
- Adopt
- Adapt

There are many examples of transformational leadership wherein change was encouraged, and such transformation has provided significant benefits to organisations. A company called Rockwell which manufactures commercial freezers was unable to cater to larger orders within the stipulated time with their existing infrastructure in 2008. Since larger orders were placed by clients only during summer, the enormous investment for permanent infrastructure expansion for higher output would be wasted. The wastage is because capacity would remain underutilised during months other than in summer.

The leadership decided to explore opportunities other than infrastructure expansion and also appointed a consultant to enable this. The consultant understood the operations in detail and realised that a lean management system was required. He identified wastage of time and effort, and suggested revision in resource planning as well as process re-engineering, which gave room for higher production. The leader showcased the benefits to the Rockwell team, and they swiftly implemented the revised process which led to 40% production increase.

The organisation not only catered for larger orders without investing in new infrastructure but also saved a lot of effort. This is a real example of transformational leadership.

FIVE

CHANGE FOR GOOD

[18] *"It is not the strongest of the species that survive, nor the most intelligent, but the ones most responsive to change."*

−**Charles Darwin.**

As per [19] Kurt Lewin, the process of change entails creating the perception that a change is needed, then moving towards the new, desired level of behaviour and, finally, solidifying that new behaviour as the norm.

To quote an example, the Indian Armed Forces regularly send select personnel, specifically officers in leadership roles, to a number of countries, like the USA and Russia for training. Similarly, many countries send their military personnel for such mid to senior level programmes. These programmes are designed to develop the officers in specific aspects of their professional knowledge. However, apart from the concepts being taught in class or during joint operations, these officers develop many other aspects of their personality, based on their experiences during the programmes. They experience diverse cultures, thoughts, procedures and practices. They appreciate and imbibe many perspectives that they never were exposed to earlier, owing to which their overall understanding of situations and decision-making quality change for the better.

It is for good reason that Indian officers, who were lucky to get that opportunity, have changed their organisational culture in a manner in which the best practices are adopted, the better traditions are retained and those 'not so good or irrelevant' ones are allowed to fade.

The officers show an enlightened edge in the handling of their professional challenges, leadership of troops and conduct of operations, all with the purpose of protecting the nation in an ever-changing internal and external environment. Such an operating environment calls for a mindset that looks at possibilities whether in managing challenges, utilising opportunities or ultimately ensuring victory during hostilities.

The above example showcases the benefit of an open mindset towards possibilities resulting in embracing change, response to change and appreciating external best practices.

Change in itself is a process that needs to be understood.

Lewin developed a change model[20] involving three steps:

- Unfreezing
- Changing
- Refreezing

This change model is relevant for organisations and employees in coping with transformation and also for leading transformation. Mindset and processes of leaders and managers have a big role to play for this to be practised. For example, adoption of the right technology is important, but the design of the process and operations, where the technology shall be put to use, is even more. Many opine that bringing in technology will give results, but unless the process has been designed well to adopt the technology including the maintenance plan, the results could be adversely impacted.

This is why planning and designing a process well initially is critical. Shortcuts at the initial stage can lead to many iterations and unnecessary costs.

Defining the purpose by an organisation aids seeking employees to connect and associate with the journey. This shift in the mindset could result in higher creativity and organisational growth.

Inspired by Aaron Sachs and Anupam Kundu, ThoughtWorks, I believe, when it comes to "leading organization transformation" that would impact the marketplace and environment, there needs to be a mindset shift:

- From the mindset of short-term goals to long-term and sustainable purpose.
- From reporting structures and hierarchies to building strong, diverse and connective networks.

- From controlled planning by senior management to empowering juniors to seek, plan and contribute.

Many large corporations like Tata group take pride in being driven by strong values and purpose. Leaders instil a deep sense of a common purpose and encourage building broad networks to mobilise efforts and resources in their teams and employees clearly witness their part in the journey.

They feel empowered to contribute since the results are gratifying.

[21] *"Business, as I have seen it, places one great demand on you: it needs you to self-impose a framework of ethics, values, fairness and objectivity on yourself at all times."*

– Ratan N Tata, 2006

Ron, a team leader of a 12-member field credit card bill collections unit that visited customers, decided to make a few changes in their work from a certain point onward. His team had been collecting for 4 years and were quite good at their work since they had developed a personal rapport with many clients. A lot of clients immediately paid when his team members visited them.

Ron felt that the team members didn't attempt to change the pattern in the customer behaviour of paying bills without a visit since it served them well. Their target was on a percentage of collection achievement on the overdue accounts allocated to them. But Ron wasn't also sure which was the exact set of customers who would pay without the visit and didn't want to risk changing the visitation strategy based on his gut and some inconclusive data. But he knew that thousands of visits could be saved, and that effort could be put onto those customers that demanded higher effort.

So, he requested his superior for an approval of an additional incentive to his team if there was a 10% reduction in repeat overdue accounts. The outcome of 8% reduction in field visits in the immediate month itself was appreciated by the leadership team.

Teams and members such as Ron seek to achieve goals, and often during that process, try to build new methods, look for opportunities and try to overcome challenges.

Certain existing methods or processes may seem confusing or complex or even lengthy. There could be many such situations wherein the teams and members come up with new solutions or products that improve upon the existing ones.

Ron's deep sense of purpose to go beyond his set check-listed scope and contribute more to the team and company needs encouragement.

However, there may be many Rons in the company whose story can be an inspiration to others in the company. So, leaders need to identify and showcase such examples of ownership. This will help build a sustainable organisation by encouraging employees to be creative and adopting the best possible practices.

Now let's understand how one transforms from the culture of hierarchies to building strong, diverse and connective networks. The influence that a certain person can exert depends on how diverse, strong and connective his or her network that has been created is! Increasing this influence increases the probability of success.

[22]Networking can be briefly defined as the art of making and maintaining relationships, which are then used for exchange of information, support and resources depending upon the need of the hour.

The network affects the ability to reach or rather the achievement opportunity of the employee and thus the organisation. What it creates is social capital (perceived value owing to the relationships).

The process of achieving goals demands an easy access to resources or information, which can also be made possible through substantial social capital.

Assessing the current network and then strategically planning towards building a well-defined network will result in a smoother path for the supervisor or manager as well as increasing chances of the team's success.

So, how does one plan and build such a network?

[23]Professor Ibarra and Hunter found in their research that "strategic networking is the ability to marshal information, support and resources from one sector of a network to achieve results in another."

Most people naturally network, but very few strategically plan their network. It is recommended that managers and supervisors plan and improve their influence by following the steps given below:

To begin with, an assessment of the current network could be done by the person, making a comprehensive list of the "go to" people – those who can be often reached for advice or contacts or for resources, etc. Then, a detailed analysis of the type of value by each person must be made. For instance, one "go to" person on the list could be a very close associate and connective, whereas another person on the list could have in-depth industry knowledge but not connective.

After mapping a type of value to each person, one could understand the composition of the entire network list.

A careful examination would clearly show the desirable values and the aspects the network lacks in. For example, the network assessment may show that there is sufficient diversity (gender/other industries, etc.), but a lower connective potential since the people in the network are less likely to create connections. So, s/he must plan the desired structured network by adding more social capital – a few more people in the "go to list" or by strengthening some relationships or reaching out to a few that can bring diversity or connective potential as seen required in the composition study.

Since, the network construct is unique to each person, strategically positioning and using the network will make goal achievement easier.

Various social and business networking mediums can be used to access resources and information, as they do provide a lot of insights on people, product and market developments. Leaders often find out that their "circle of influence" is greater than they had thought it to be.

SIX

CULTURE OF INNOVATING

While curiosity is considered the mother of inventions, it is believed that ownership plays an important role too.

Many a time, certain processes are just followed by employees since they have been a part of the approved checklist while some aspects of the process or practices may have become ineffective or obsolete. So, there is a need for reviewing processes and practices regularly and finding alternative options that could be employed to improve output.

In most organisations, strategy is worked upon, reviewed and built in the high quarters of a corporate office who may or may not have worked enough on the process themselves. At best, some of them would have worked directly years ago on those processes, some reviewed the processes, and some learnt the concepts in classrooms.

Now, the questions thus are:

Who are the ones in the best position to understand and comment on existing processes?

Who faces and understands the loopholes or challenges?

Who has higher chances to come up with alternatives?

Strategy and Planning without involving ground operations in true spirit is not ideal since innovations don't always happen at the workspace as an outcome of a planned effort to innovate by seniors.

Firstly, the need for a culture of innovating needs to be understood.

Some are:

- To improve efficiencies
- To change external environment
- To change current operations that may nct fuel growth for long
- To ideate
- To create new avenues or solutions

More often than not, inspiration, constraints and high passion lead to innovations. Such a culture of conscious creativity should be recognised, encouraged and amplified. But as written about earlier in the book, many employees may fear speaking up even if they have ideas or suggestions and don't want to risk negative perception, which is an unwanted culture. An open organisation which recognises and values seeking and employee participation encourages people to speak up and discourages labelling.

This culture of seeking and participation can also be propagated by organising an "Idea or Innovation Week" or a platform for showcasing unique and creative methods of learnings and achievements at work.

Especially in such a dynamic external environment, seeking employees and psychologically safe teams can propel organisations with innovative ways.

Broadly, there are 2 types of innovations.

- Sustaining innovations: Those that help the performance of an existing product, network with the existing market customers and methods; basically, do more with less.

- Disruptive innovations: Those that replace existing methods or products or radically change the market and value of the products.

Sustaining innovations in all organisations happens during the continuous improvement cycle of existing products and processes to achieve higher efficiency.

> [24] *"The less an organization has to do to produce results, the better it does its job."*
>
> **– Peter F. Drucker**

A factor influencing such innovations is the ownership drive towards excellence and achievement.

The other important factor is working with constraints related to input, workspace, demand, supply, etc.

Most organisations innovate on some level but highly transformational organisations with an employee culture of high seeking and learning quotient have a higher success rate in developing disruptive innovations. Leaders, with a high drive for leading transformation in extremely competitive environments, plan and strive for disruptive innovations.

While organisations focus on innovation, historically, it has been noted that certain kinds of innovations have led to making investments without an in-depth understanding of the need, potential and impact. Such organisations have suffered losses and damages.

On the other hand, many companies have catapulted themselves to highly successful ones owing to the innovations they worked upon and implemented well.

During the times of COVID-19, a lot of people under lockdown and quarantine started spending so much more time either alone or with their families. Many responded to this situation by devising creative ways to engage children, work from home, outsource, conserve, collaborate, etc. These constraints actually forced people and organisations to strive and find innovative ways.

During the same period, Cult.fit highly popularised their e-fit class option and got thousands of members staying home to use their app to do their fitness class, while most other fitness centres shut indefinitely.

Cult.fit centres which started in 2017 became a big rage in urban India, as fitness enthusiasts saw value in multiple options of interesting and fun-based work-outs like boxing, football, yoga, dance, high intensity training, etc. in one Cult.fit centre, with the flexibility of booking any class and not having to stick to a particular one every day.

This range of options motivated them to join Cult.fit instead of the conventional gymnasium.

The cherry on top was the highly interactive mobile application which Cult.fit developed, that allowed selection from choice of type of session and time slot in advance. This suited working professionals well. As some might find it difficult to physically go to the centre every single day, owing to traffic conditions or hectic schedules or even frequent travel, Cult.fit offered an "e-fit" option from 2019. This led to them taking online workout, therapy sessions, meditations, yoga, etc. to a whole new level.

The journey of Cult.fit goes to show that organisations, primarily, should believe that every need can be satisfied and any convenience can be created. All it takes is a strong will that needs to be encouraged.

Examples of disruptive innovations are: how Google revolutionised email, travel with Google Maps, learning through Google search, etc. Kindle made reading easier, turning books into entities to be carried anywhere and everywhere. GE Medical systems came up with kid friendly MRI machines.

Teams should be made to understand the scope of benefits for consumers and have faith that they can make innovations happen, to enable improvement in efficiency, convenience and output. With this school of thought being followed, any and every relevant opportunity would be explored by employees. Innovations are not limited to technology. With the advancement and adoption of technology, it seems like innovations and advancement will be in technology going forward. But we should understand that the larger picture is beyond technology, as the market landscape is always changing. IOT, gig, farm direct, mobile banking, plant-based meat products and organic food adoption patterns are proving that remote working, remote management, human skill development, consumption patterns and logistical advancement may be the change drivers. A marginal improvement of per capita income of smaller cities can domino into a large shift especially in the case of infrastructure, logistics and consumption. It may happen that work migration patterns change and consumption in smaller towns and even villages significantly increases. Therefore, closely monitoring and studying the customer, market and product trends could give great insights and the edge to bridge and capitalise on new opportunities.

Now that we have understood the possibilities and impact of innovating, let's dive into the most common strategies[25] that organisations invest in selectively or as a process:

- Need seeker: Increased or exclusive focus on customer
- Market reader: Increased or exclusive focus understanding the market dynamics
- Technology or product driver: Increased or exclusive focus on product, process or technology

Investment in such dedicated efforts are highly recommended for organisations that deal with dynamic environments and highly competitive landscapes. It is also very essential to lead transformation.

After identifying the need/dynamics/drivers suited to the desired transformation, it is important to design the probable solution and test the outcome.

Sometimes, leaders take adoption by teams as a given thinking that teams understand the benefits. They may not invest enough effort for readying the teams and infrastructure which can potentially impact operations. Leaders need to be conscious of readiness, adoption and change.

A RECAP OF THE KEY POINTS COVERED

- Transformational needs and leadership
- Purposeful change necessary for sustained growth
- Strategic building of networks
- Types of innovation and the method of innovating

KEY TAKE-AWAYS

ACTION PLANS

_____

_____

_____

_____

_____

_____

_____

_____

_____

_____

_____

_____

_____

SECTION 3

Performance and Talent Assessment

*S*imon, an aspirational leader of a software service company, met with the managers of his team one morning. He informed them of the need to improve the size of their client base serviced by them significantly while planning for the year ahead. He believed that the revenue would proportionately grow, and it was a fair strategy to concentrate on acquisition instead of the ticket size.

They brainstormed together to arrive at a business plan:

- Acquisition target of two clients per month and
- Hiring two engineers per month to service the projected new client base

However, Simon was worried about the employee attrition of 30% which was due to poor loyalty according to him. He was thus burdened with the need to fill the future attrition in addition to the mighty hiring projection.

The managers often complained that the service engineers didn't care about the struggle to meet client expectations. They said that SEs didn't care much for the outcome even though the managers spent a lot of time teaching them various aspects of project management and client engagement.

Based on repeated complaints from managers, Simon started to believe that employees were mere tools and that client management was the real job, as it was often he who ended up fixing issues.

With this understanding, he decided to do the following:

- *He would focus on client acquisition himself*
- *He would personally work on tie-ups with 2 colleges for campus recruitment, in order to meet the next year's budgeted service plan*
- *He would delegate the job of fixing operational problems to the 3 managers*
- *Tell the managers that the 3 of them have to keep clients engaged and keep striving to find new ways while pushing the limits since service engineers will always be low on engagement*

From everything that has been discussed in this example until now, one would derive that the probability of him achieving his projected plan is very low.

Some of the key failure points in this strategy are:

- Lack of direction or of a platform that provides insights on planning and progress for the teams to associate with journey.
- Onus of scaling business only with Simon.
- Focus on project-based planning instead of building organisation capability.
- Lack of an engagement improvement plan for the service engineers.
- Service engineer's disassociation with outcomes due to manager's inability to establish accountability with the team.

The next few chapters will help understand how one could create ownership, empower team members, assess talent/competencies/achievements and make people decisions.

SEVEN

MILESTONES AND CONTINUOUS ASSESSMENT!

The vision of the organisation could be laid out or broken down in the form of long-term, medium-term and short-term goals. Since "time" is a very important resource and it keeps ticking away, strategic planning of work in time phases and milestones gives the opportunity for effectively managing progress.

For defining organisational goals, the leader first needs to build a detailed roadmap with key imperatives or milestones from the current position to the point when vision is successfully achieved. At times, it may prove to be more beneficial to have three or four road maps, in which each of them represents a goal.

It is prudent to create goals that are SMART:

- **S**pecific
- **M**easurable
- **A**chievable

- **R**elevant
- **T**imebound

Setting SMART goals is an important exercise that gives clear direction and expectation by the leader in the very beginning to the employees. One needs to be aware that too many goals will be difficult to prioritise, track and manage. Therefore, it is recommended not to set more than 6 goals for the journey.

In the previous example, Simon had set very limited goals. Client satisfaction score and employee attrition targets for managers were completely missed. He could have tried to define goals using the SMART method for the employees.

After finalising the goals, assigning them to teams is the next process. Employees' goals and expectations have to tie in with the organisation's goals and plans. For example, the CEO's goals get broken down into goals of functional heads and then split further into goals of managers and so on.

The following steps are recommended for achievement of goals:

- Breaking of each goal into work plans by employees
- Setting a charter for managing progress closely to review, support or resolve challenges that may arise
- Facilitating teams with a platform for assessment of goals

[26] *"Good leaders make people feel that they're at the very heart of things, not at the periphery."*

– Warren Bennis

By including employees in the process of defining and delegating goals, it becomes clear across the organisation that the leadership believes and acknowledges that employees are an integral part of the journey, and setting expectations upfront gives clarity, reduces confusion and anxiety. Also, a person's ownership quotient is higher when he or she associates themselves with the journey and explores the path.

Unfortunately, many a time, the employee is unable to see value in tasks or goals assigned to them, as they can't associate with the purpose and tend to undermine the importance of the goals and tasks to self or organisation. Therefore, it falls upon the leader or supervisor to explain in detail the criticality and purpose of the assigned goal while assigning it to a particular employee or team.

When employees are encouraged to create work plans to achieve goals, they start exploring ways of achievement instead of being assigned miniscule tasks.

After work plans are set by employees, the supervisor needs to do regular check-ins on the individual's progress of work plans, preferably on a weekly or fortnightly timeline, to support or help resolve challenges if any.

GOAL MANAGEMENT

(Exhibit 7)

GOALS
Set goals and sub goals.

WORK PLANNING
Each goal could be broken into work plans by the Individual.

CHECK-INS
Individual records challenges and the support needed.

REGULAR INETERACTIVE
Regular weekly updates by Individual get reviewed by the manager.

READY FOR ASSESSMENT
The progress summary of sub goals and workplans help individual and manager for an Informed appraisal

Generally, this should not take over 5-10 mins on an average per individual for the supervisor each time. Such a practice gives visibility to the supervisor on the progress and also provides an opportunity to support the team members in a structured way.

This culture of work planning builds ownership in the employees and empowers them to explore facts, look at options and decide on methods suitable.

In a nutshell, if each goal is broken down into structured work plans by the employee under the guidance of the supervisor, the employees associate themselves with the organisation's journey. Achievement of these work plans and sub goals effectively facilitate timely achievement of goals. And instead of only rewarding employees based on achievement, rewarding employees also based on effort and strategy would create an environment where employees will own their work and actively engage themselves through the process.

After the work plans are created and the progress is regularly managed by supervisors, it is important for leadership to facilitate continuous assessment.

[27] *"What gets measured gets improved."*

– Peter F. Drucker

As per Dr MP Ganesh[28], Cognitive biases of the evaluators can seriously hamper the efficacy of employee performance evaluations. Most of this can be avoided when the evaluators are trained to be cognizant of these biases and also through continuous assessment of employee performance.

It is surprising but true that some organisations avoided rating employee performance and gave a standard raise to all employees, taking into consideration the industry pay-scale and company performance.

While the advantage of having a standard/fixed pay increase is that there will be no conflict of bias, it is often construed by employees that merit or excellence is not being valued within the organisation.

Few other organisations did assessments only to decide salary increases but do not use the assessments for people development and as a process of providing valuable feedback to employees.

Regular performance review and feedback are necessary, and such reviews would help employees and managers gain understanding of their own progress. Organisations use the output of review for planning employee developmental initiatives and careers.

A flawed practice that needs to be discouraged is leaders tending to refer to the most recent performance and potential of the employee, while rating and recognising them during the annual assessment cycle.

A defined frequency of assessment sets realistic expectation and accountability. A process of half yearly assessment supported with regular check-ins by the supervisor to ratify the work plans and resolve their challenges will be effective and also construed to be a fair assessment, not giving room for recency effect.

However, this process is best implemented and managed by using a goal management platform.

EIGHT

UNDERSTANDING AND DEVELOPING TALENT

An employee's performance against goals, while very important, does not indicate his or her managerial capability. High performance does not necessarily mean that the employee could ably handle larger responsibilities or larger teams. So, in addition to performance assessment, organisations should understand and plan development of talent.

Leadership needs to understand various dimensions apart from performance of employees since:

- Not all employees fit a specific process or job
- Their potential and capabilities vary
- Some realise their potential on their own while some seek direction in order to do so
- Some perform well within a certain framework
- They come with varied strengths and development needs

Leaders must review the talent of the organisation to make informed people decisions. The talent review output should be reviewed holistically by the leadership taking into consideration development of employees and the organisation's growth plans.

With the help of the talent review, they can build a 6 to12 month roadmap and plan specific types of investment (time, effort and/or money) if needed against each employee or set of employees (generally above a grade or those in supervisory roles) pertaining to:

- Performance and potential development
- Succession
- Retention
- Career progression and rewards
- Job fitment

Generally, the achievement of the past 6 or 12 months is considered as performance whereas what the employee will be able to deliver or contribute in the future is considered as potential. It not only includes the potential to perform in the current role, but also the ability to perform at a higher role. Potential additionally includes certain attributes like influence and capacity of the employee that are changing for better or worse.

Lalita has been the team leader of a 6-member team for 2 years. In the recently held talent review, it was assessed that Lalita is showing potential to handle a larger responsibility and team.

On the other hand, Raveena, who has been team leader for 3 years of a similar team, was assessed to be low on potential since her team management skills needed to improve.

It was also assessed in the talent review that the client engagement quality needed improvement in the case of Frank, the project lead, while he performed well.

It is very important for an organisation to understand the various dimensions pertaining to the employees.

DIMENSIONS OF TALENT MANAGEMENT

(Exhibit 8)

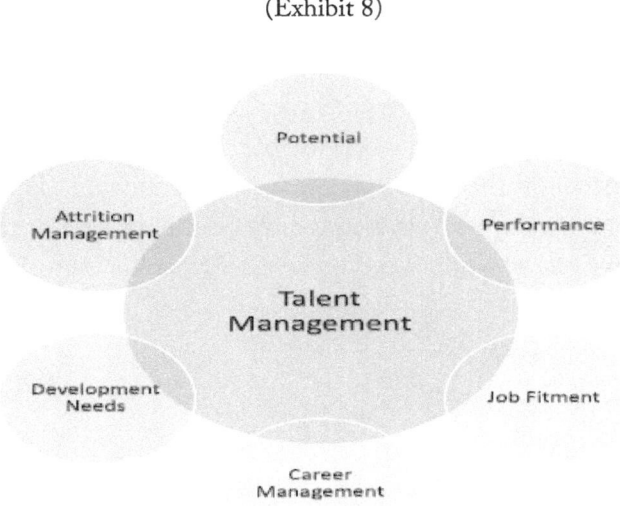

Based on the assessment of strengths, weaknesses and development areas, the organisation plans training and other employee developmental initiatives. Employees' strengths can be nurtured to positively impact growth of the individual and the organisation. Similarly, employees with development areas may need training, mentoring and/or upskilling in the identified areas.

It is important to also understand the probability of an employee leaving the organisation in the foreseeable future based on certain behavioural traits, performance or information. Subsequently, leaders need to assess the probable impact if attrition does take place. Based on the probability of attrition and the impact of attrition, the organisation needs to plan the next steps for eventualities such as retention and succession for specific employees. Plans should be in place for certain positions by virtue of importance or those which can't be easily substituted or filled in. And, if the impact of the projected attrition of a specific individual is very low, the organisation needs to review whether it is low because of job fitment or because the need of the position itself is questionable. There may be employees better suited for another role over the current role so understanding of job fitment is important too.

NINE

COMPETENCIES

Assessing and developing competencies would greatly help employees improve their performance.

Different employees in the team display different competencies and behaviours. One's competencies and behaviours at work have an impact on performance of colleagues and work processes too.

Most of the time, organisations define competencies and behaviours expected from employees at work and work processes. But, merely defining the expected behaviours is not sufficient. It is imperative that the gaps are identified, and the bar is raised.

It is highly recommended for organisations to establish a method to analyse employees' competencies and behaviours at least annually.

Ideally, competency assessment could be done by employing a:

- 180-degree evaluation – involving the employee and seniors (including supervisor) or

- 270-degree evaluation – involving the employee, seniors and subordinates or

- 360-degree evaluation – involving the employee, seniors, peers and subordinates

The evaluation could be done by using a simple questionnaire and/or vignettes and/or a situation analysis.

The results could be mapped onto the competency scale or Behaviourally Anchored Rating Scale (BARS)[29].

Exhibit 9 illustrates how the levels could be defined for one of the competencies:

BARS for Customer Service Orientation – (Exhibit 9) - An example	
Competency BARS/Levels	Definition
L1	Enquire and collect relevant details from the customer.
L2	Maintains clear communication with the client regarding mutual expectations.
L3	Creates personalisation in offerings to meet customer needs.
L4	Follows up empathetically on customer issues, changing needs and performance.
L5	Takes personal responsibility for customer satisfaction and success.

The evaluation of the employee will determine the current level of the competency. If the current level is found to be L2 for the competency but the desired level predetermined as per the organisation for the role is L3, the gap of development need is clearly identified.

The process of filling the gap requires the employee to go through the process of learning or upskilling. Organisations can push curated content pertaining to the specific gap and could also arrange for onsite training as per need.

An example: Summary of Nurse Annie's evaluation

(Exhibit 10)

LEVELS	EXAMPLE- COMPETENCIES SCORECARD			
	Technical	**Ownership**	**Empathy**	**Communication**
L1				
L2	▓			▓
L3		▓		
L4			▓	

A hospital that assesses employees using such a scorecard could help improve the overall patient engagement score.

As per this example of competency assessment scorecard, the nurses are required to focus on technical competencies such as checking vitals and maintaining patient records. They are also expected to display empathy, high ownership and communicate properly with doctors, colleagues and patients.

A summary of this type of evaluation as seen in Exhibit 10 for all the nurses would help identify every individual's exact development area and training needs. Training the nurses on the identified gap will ensure addressing the right need and provide the specific development.

In this manner, employing or developing a competency framework and tool could help the organisation assess competencies and seamlessly fill gaps.

Such a competency evaluation could also be used for identifying candidates during recruitment and internal job changes.

Supervisors need to understand that competency assessment and development of their teams are on-going processes that need to be consciously worked upon.

Some of the examples of development needs are:

- Personal and interpersonal development like emotional quotient, anxiety, anger, empathy, self-confidence, active-listening and ability to accept constructive feedback
- Analytical skill development like mathematics, computing and planning
- Strong communication and persuasiveness
- Managerial and leadership skills like collaboration, empowering, delegation and decision-making
- Creativity

It is not possible for every employee to possess all the above skills and abilities, but a lack of the skills and proficiencies relevant to the job delegated needs to be identified and addressed.

A RECAP OF THE POINTS COVERED IN THIS CHAPTER

- Goal management
- The culture of work planning
- Talent assessment and development
- Appraising employee performance
- Defining and assessing of competencies and their development

KEY TAKE-AWAYS

ACTION PLANS

_____

_____

_____

_____

_____

_____

_____

_____

_____

_____

_____

_____

_____

_____

_____

_____

SECTION 4

Managing Self While Managing Teams

Prof. Herminia Ibarra in her book *Act Like a Leader, Think Like a Leader*[30] explains that it is often easy for leaders to slip into competency traps when they enjoy what they do well a bit too much and end up doing more of it. And when they allot more time to things they already do best and devote less time to things they don't really like or are not too good at, their understanding becomes narrow and may miss learning other things that are essential to achievement of goals.

One needs to devote time to four tasks to act like a leader and avoid being in the competency trap:

- Bridging across diverse people and groups
- Envisioning new possibilities
- Engaging people in the process of change
- Embodying the change

This way, the leader can focus on developing great talent in the organisation and a platform for them to connect on work needs, exchange information and share possibilities, enabling growth.

The leader needs to build fearless energy and enhance capabilities recognising collaboration, creativity and achievement.

[31] *"Courage is the power of the mind to overcome fear."*

– **Martin Luther King Jr.**

This section helps understand aspects pertaining to supervisory influence on team members and how the supervisors/ leaders need to manage their own conduct, dichotomies and biases so that their influence fuels growth and harmony in the organisation.

It also covers the way leaders could build an enterprise that values guidance.

TEN

THE SUPERVISOR'S INFLUENCE

The extent of influence that supervisors are capable of exerting on those they manage is immense. If this influence of the supervisor is constructive providing direction as well as support to the employee, the team and organisation shall benefit.

The supervisor's texture of handling his/ her own position and prerogative comes across in various ways.

- How effectively do they interact with their team?
- Are they aware of the style of management they employ?
- What is the impact of their working dynamics on teams, working partners like vendors and other colleagues?

As seen in the first part, successful leaders build and encourage great relationships.

A lot depends on the conviction with which managers and supervisors shift often between playing different roles such as being a guide, a coach and delegating while dealing with their team members. All this while holding them accountable for the goal.

The exclusive goal check-ins, discussed earlier, to be performed by supervisors in predetermined regular intervals, should not be diluted by digressing into other company matters during the check-in. Through these check-ins, supervisors need to look for signs if someone needs help or is trying to avoid difficult situations and challenges.

While it is with growth mindset that one embraces challenges, supervisors ensure focus is not lost and help team members with clarity when the members find it challenging to plan.

[32]GROW MODEL

(Exhibit 11)

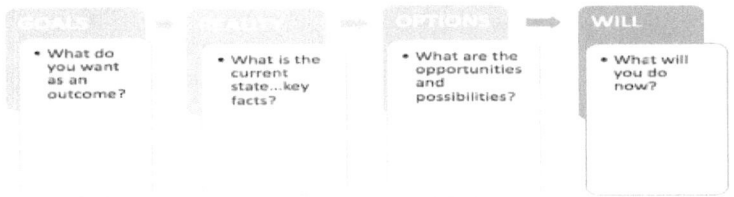

For this, the supervisor could employ the GROW model to unlock the potential or maximise performance.

GROW is a step by step process that is commonly used by business leaders but is exclusive, as it is only through a one-on-one session. This model, as seen in Exhibit 11, simplifies the complexity of the issue with the aid of a sequential questioning method – what is the need? What is the current state? What are the options? And then finally, what will you do now?

[33]*"A boss has the title; a leader has the people."*

– Simon Sinek

During this process, the supervisor plays the role of an active listener, displaying patience and empathy without indulging in directly telling the employee what to do. Instead, s/he leads the employee down the path of discovering further steps that are required in order to achieve the desired goal. They establish clear lines of communication, spreading joy, embracing optimism and positive thinking to build confidence in workplaces.

They practice humility, respect and trust while encouraging team members to do the same.

During their discussions, supervisors could start by referring to the goals and expectations previously assigned, enquire of the progress made, listen intently taking note of the support if needed, and finally, motivate and coach.

Supervisors need to be aware of their impact on teams and in managing performance discussions.

Managing performance discussions (Exhibit 12)

MANAGING PERFORMANCE DISCUSSIONS

(Exhibit 12)

Maya worked with a bank in Mumbai. She liked her job, was actively engaged in her work and was a good performer. Being a single mother, she needed to be home by 7.30 pm from work and so found it difficult to cope with attending the evening meetings being called for post office hours on a regular basis; especially, if not given sufficient notice by her boss, Ravi.

Many a time, Maya contemplated calling Ravi to explain her situation in detail but found it difficult to even make that happen since he didn't seem approachable. On his part, Ravi rarely held any one-on-one discussion with his team members regarding the issues they may be facing at work.

Maya decided to quit her job.

Managers and supervisors should plan ahead and be prepared for performance discussions with their members during the assessment cycle and for the check-ins. These discussions are also opportunities for improving motivation levels and engagement quotient of the team members.

The supervisors need to first understand their team members and the situations they are in well. Maya would have been further motivated if her boss understood and empathised with her. Regular discussions would have made that possible, and Maya would not have left the organisation.

The 360-degree feedback and evaluation framework would help Ravi identify his blind spot/s in such a situation. If Ravi had been aware of his people management style and EQ (emotional quotient), he would have been conscious about the aspects he needs to work upon and may have actively listened, empathised and taken note of the issue Maya was facing.

360-DEGREE FEEDBACK SYSTEM

(Exhibit 13)

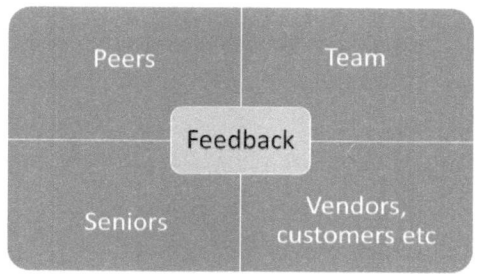

Supervisors can seek constructive feedback from their colleagues (seniors, juniors, peers and customers) who work closely with them as seen in Exhibit 13. The feedback could help supervisors introspect about various aspects of their engagement and management.

Often managers are under the impression that their EQ[34] (Emotional Quotient) with their teams is great, only to find out that their teams actually scored them low on EQ. It is therefore necessary to adopt regular interactive sessions to manage this.

Being in denial of their blind spots is a trap that leaders often fall into, but they need to be open to feedback and understand that EQ is one of the most important elements in managing people and high EQ supervisors have a higher chance to progress in an organisation.

It is to be noted that leaders possessing high empathy and control over impulses are more likely to develop successful teams.

While enhancing EQ may take months of patience, commitment and determination, the results are worth it.

[35]The author of *Business Sutra*, Devdutt Pattanaik explains in the book about different cultures and people from different regions having different philosophies of seeking. In this context, he also speaks of the distinction between Objectivity and Subjectivity. It may be a good idea to understand opinions and appreciate the diversity.

There is no one way to seek really – each person is unique with a different set of experiences. Both people and situations can be complex and perceptions of people to those situations matter.

These varied perceptions introduce an element of subjectivity. So, understanding people and their intent will help supervisors in mentoring or guiding the members better. The universe is full of possibilities, but many people are comfortable to make things as objective as possible since it is easier to manage if the scope of employee's work is reduced to task fulfilment only.

But such a narrow outlook could stifle creativity, and employees may find their jobs less purposeful.

When we start appreciating diversity, our minds expand and see possibilities beyond the obvious.

Team leaders and managers who build open work cultures and appreciate people for their unique perspectives, encourage sharing of thoughts and experiences.

[36]According to Daniel Goleman, a fine balance between the "thinking brain" and the "feeling brain" gives immense clarity in how a certain situation or individual can be handled.

Emotional intelligence impacts everyday life and every decision one makes. Anyone is susceptible to making flawed decisions at times, as decisions are aided not only by logic, but also by memory, reference and experience.

An example from a football field that I heard of seems apt here – a footballer did not pass the ball to a player on his team who was strategically placed to receive the pass and score the goal, as he recalled the player missing a similar pass earlier in the year. He did not take into account that there had been a significant improvement in the teammate's game recently.

An aspiring leader must develop an awareness of how feelings influence action and thought, as this consciousness would aid greatly in managing emotions.

However, it is not so simple because of the demand to manage simultaneous action plans while leading and maintaining harmony within teams.

Communicating well aids this process.

The connection between the leader and his employees grows only when the subordinates feel involved in finding solutions, and at times, they may surprise their leader with great finds.

ELEVEN

MANAGING DICHOTOMIES

Jocko Willink[37], a navy seal and the author of *Leadership Strategy and Tactics* explains that leaders often face many dichotomies (defined as a sharp division of things or ideas into two contradictory parts) and should practice balance.

Leaders should be able to practice balance while dealing with teams especially while communicating and demanding discipline.

Leaders should help teams feel humility, mutual respect and togetherness, but also hold them accountable and employ disciplinary action in case of extreme scenarios.

So how does one learn to manage these many and different dichotomies?

Leaders and managers gain respect by displaying high levels of ownership and willingness to own the outcome. Ultimately, the responsibility lies on the leader's shoulders, and they must learn to prioritise between personal success and team glory. In doing so, managing one's own ego becomes important. One should not be pretentious and definitely not behave like a know-all.

Leaders should also ensure that everyone that belongs to the team feels that their role is essential to the success of the team.

A true leader must never be afraid to apologise, as acknowledging one's mistakes goes a long way in gaining respect and setting an example of ownership to the members of the team. Similarly, in the event of having to penalise someone in the team, they need to be aware that failure was under their command and that a team member's failures reflect on their training effectiveness or communication on the role.

While creating and holding employees accountable for work, micro-managing could mean that you don't trust that team member's capability. To counter this, the leader must ask questions, guiding people in a direction that would help solve problems on their own. The leader must refrain from solving each and every problem that arises.

When team members are involved in drawing up plans for the task, it creates a culture of ownership. If the plan that the team has suggested has a high probability of working, they could be rewarded by giving a go-ahead to that particular plan.

In order to stay relevant, leaders have to work towards becoming adept with communication skills and must employ them in the following ways:

- Ensure praise is balanced and specific
- Use affirmation to motivate teams
- Use a proactive approach of updating progress
- Provide regular feedback to strengthen the ownership quotient
- Ensure no one feels ignored when communicating with teams by establishing clear lines of communication avoiding rumours which can impact the motivation levels of other employees
- Seek feedback and suggestions so that the process of communication doesn't become one-sided
- Be proactive and responsive to avoid delays and develop a greater circle of influence

Being conscious from the time of stimuli to the final response makes a world of difference as quality of response plays an important role, and so, being hasty in responding is not healthy. It would help to set expectations such as an approximate response time for a specific type of response and communicate well to avoid anxiousness in teams.

TWELVE

BELIEFS AND ACTION

It is the belief in one's own capability that drives the person. Once a path becomes clear or when the path seems familiar, one's confidence that achievement is possible rises significantly. But, the expectations of others that one is surrounded by also drives the person.

The Pygmalion effect[38] is a phenomenon which explains that the greater the expectation placed upon people, the higher the impact, and the chances of them performing well also increase.

The Pygmalion effect is also called the Rosenthal effect. [39]Robert Rosenthal, a professor of psychology, was known for his self-fulfilling prophecies focusing on the effects of expectations.

[40]According to a Harvard business review, if a leader believes in the capabilities of the members of his/her team, they will reliably outperform a group whose leader believes the opposite – even if the innate talent of the two groups are similar.

Exhibit 14

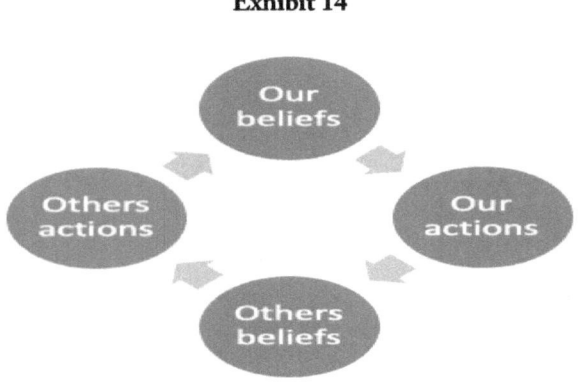

Our beliefs influence our actions towards others. Our actions impact others' beliefs about their capability. Their beliefs cause their actions towards results and finally their actions reinforce our original beliefs.

The Pygmalion effect can also be seen and explained by another simple example.

If a teacher tells a student that he or she is not good in Physics, the student will eventually believe the same and may even stop trying to get better, resulting in bad grades, which only proves the primary belief of the teacher that the student is not good in Physics.

On the other hand, if the teacher would have told the student that he or she is good in the subject, he or she will eventually believe the same. The student with that belief, studies to meet the expectation of the teacher and scores well. This success reinforces the initial belief of the teacher.

Certain expectations set by some supervisors towards some employees over others have instilled belief in those employees, and they have worked towards achievement with the aided motivation to meet expectation and succeed. This shows how impactful the leader's verbal and non-verbal communication would be on the subordinate.

Some leaders tend to believe more in some team members than they do in others and set corresponding expectations for them. Because of this belief, the leader focuses on these team members to help them achieve, leading to the possibility that they produce better results. This in turn reinforces the initial belief system of the leader.

The Pygmalion phenomenon goes to show that the supervisor can influence the progress of teams significantly. But it also throws light upon the need for supervisors and leaders to be mindful of initial predetermined beliefs which could prove detrimental for the team. The supervisor has to avoid predetermined beliefs and understand all his/her subordinates before forming individual action plans for them.

KEY ASPECTS COVERED IN THIS CHAPTER

- Managing performance discussions
- Receiving constructive feedback
- Building EQ
- Balance in communication
- The impact of expectations

KEY TAKE-AWAYS

_____

_____

_____

_____

_____

_____

_____

_____

_____

_____

_____

_____

_____

_____

ACTION PLANS

_____

_____

_____

_____

_____

_____

_____

_____

_____

_____

_____

_____

_____

SECTION 5

Workplace Synergies

[41] Devdutt Pattanaik in his book *Business Sutra* explains that if it is believed that wealth needs to be chased, the workplace becomes a *rana-bhoomi* – a battleground of investors, regulators, employers, employees, vendors, competitors and customers; on the other hand, if it is believed that wealth needs to be attracted, the workplace becomes a *ranga-bhoomi* – a playground where everyone is happy.

One can apply the above not just to wealth, but also to success. Also, it is completely up to the leaders and managers to make the workplace either a *rana-bhoomi* or *ranga-bhoomi*.

This part of the book covers some of the synergies at the workplace that are responsible for harmony and a sense of belonging.

THE BEGINNING

*F*resh off campus, 9 newly placed management trainees reached TAC CORP for their first day at work. They were nervous while sitting in the reception, but excited to see how their workplace was, and above all this, curious to know what was in store for them.

Soon the HR manager met with them and after a brief greeting led them to a large conference room.

They were surprised to see 5 leadership team members seated inside including the CEO.

Following a round of introductions with the leadership, the CEO gave a snapshot of the history and key landmarks of the company. The 9 of them were welcomed to introduce their best selves along with an instance that described it; all of it within 5 minutes. Each of them narrated some instance or event that they felt proud of while the rest of the people heard the introduction and stories intently.

The HR leader explained the organisation's values and behaviours and gave them a flavour of the organisation's culture. She then introduced each of them to their mentors for *the subsequent 3 months. After the leadership team left, the induction itinerary and project schedule for the 3 months was given to them by the HR manager.*

The new joiners expected that they would be greeted at best by the HR head and be introduced to the HR practices or policies on their first day. Instead, they left office that evening feeling special and looking forward to making a great start, remembering each other by wonderful stories. This made for great bonding between them.

The quality of the induction defines the employee's outlook of the organisation, processes and also sets a sense of belonging.

A good induction process focuses on motivating the employee and provides a well-summarised introduction of the organisation, its culture, and people, apart from the processes. By the end of the induction, it is important they feel emotionally connected with the organisation and empowered on a path to succeed.

[42]Dr Dweck emphasises that no matter what the level of one's current ability, effort ignites that ability and moulds it towards accomplishment.

Hence, effort is an essential component in the process of cultivating talent, and motivation needs to be a continuous process right from the time of employee's induction.

The induction should not seem like it is a check-listed process. By the end of the induction, they should see themselves ready, excited and poised to be entrusted with valuable responsibilities.

The key pointers to be taken note of at this stage are the following:

Firstly, it is best that a senior leader does a short session with the management trainees introducing the organisation and explaining how joining the organisation opens doors towards a wonderful journey for each one of them.

[43]Professor Daniel Cable says that new hires should be encouraged to introduce their best selves by describing an event that they are proud of to the other hires apart from their basic introduction. Employees will start relating with each other's stories and best selves leading to bonding and a positive work environment.

Further, assignment of mentors to new hires as part of the induction process will ensure support and guidance since some of them may lack confidence and courage in different phases of the initial months with the company. A mentor would generally be a senior manager or part of the leadership team and would spend an hour every week with the management trainees during the first 3 months.

There should be a specifically designed programme to introduce the relevant processes and people, in order to ensure that employees don't end up in the units without sufficient knowledge since unit members may not be equipped or have the time to introduce or train the employee while on job.

At this stage, the goals are assigned, and the employee starts with the work planning process as described in the part "Performance and Talent Assessment" in this book.

While this is the case of management trainees, every employee who joins the organisation needs to feel important to the organisation's growth journey. HR should facilitate an induction that helps them associate with the organisation.

LIGHT UP THE DARK CORNER

*K*han has been managing a dedicated team of twelve members, in the capacity of an Assistant Manager with a Telecom company for 3 years.

Their mainstay was resolving billing complaints, and the team dealt with customers who raised billing queries and complaints. Each team member handled an average of a hundred queries daily, and they managed to resolve 80% of the queries immediately. The resolution of balance 20% took 28 hours on an average, in order to understand the issue in-depth and facilitate support from other departments.

Romit, the new billing department head, received a request from Khan for an additional team member owing to the 10% increase in the customer queries and complaints. While Romit empathised with the team for handling the additional load, he met with the teams involved in customer query registration and resolution to understand the reason for the increase in complaints and queries, which his predecessor had not done.

He understood the following after studying the data, speaking with the team and listening to sample calls:

- *40% of the queries were pertaining to payment methods and duplicate bill requests since they were not aware of the bill or payment method/options and enquired about the same.*

- *The team emailed bill copies to customers while on call when they understood that the request was for a bill.*

Romit came up with the following solutions:

- *Sales team to explain the payment options and hand over a FAQs leaflet at the time of new sale.*

- *Provided duplicate bill e-dispatch rights to all customer-facing employees encountering such queries.*

- *Message to existing customers asking for confirmation of their registered email id and contact details so that bills are sent to right contacts.*

- *Highlight the payment options and insert payment links prominently in the bills instead of bill simply mentioning to refer to the website for payment options.*

By implementing the above steps, the billing queries had come down by 18%, and also an improvement was recorded in the % of early payers in the subsequent month.

On many occasions, it so happens that the problems faced by employees on the ground are not the ones being worked upon in the Corporate Head office.

Many leaders and managers assume that they understand the issues plaguing their teams and start working for solutions without understanding the needs of the employees that are working real time.

At the other end, many team members assume that their managers are aware of the problems to be encountered and end up not discussing them. Moreover, they also assume that their managers are already working on them, or that such issues are part of the normal course. Another observation in workplaces is that teams don't feel empowered enough to raise certain issues with their superiors.

It must be established that challenges of individuals are best known when faced and at times are unique too. Therefore, it is imperative that all kinds of challenges receive the deserved attention at all levels of the organisation.

Leaders should be aware that team members may be sceptical to talk about the challenges they face. They also may attempt to impress their managers by describing only the efforts being made by them and not bring up problems. It is important that teams feel empowered to own and call out for help pertaining to challenges faced, no matter how small. Work plan check-ins are not complete without identifying the key challenges faced by teams and providing them with necessary support. Tracking progress should be more for helping individuals with direction and providing support than just identifying the gap between current status and projected status.

Leaders should involve the teams while making strategic plans. Teams help leaders understand ground needs and showcase the opportunities that leaders may not be aware of. Similarly, the team's sense of purpose tends to be high while executing plans if they are involved in planning.

FIFTEEN

CREATING SYNERGY AMONGST TEAMS

One of the reasons for failure of most cross-functional teams is that units work in silos. For example, the production team may not work well with the tech team.

Generally, employees within a function or unit have good synergy since they have common goals and understand the progress of the unit well. Sometimes, they look at other functions or units as their competition and remain agnostic to the growth of others.

A confectionary that makes biscuits and chocolates didn't meet its yearly plan mainly due to a dip in turnover of the biscuits in February and March.

During the review, the sales head blamed the production head, and subsequently, the production team shifted the blame on to the procurement team saying that sufficient quantity of flour was not procured by them. The procurement team justified that the flour supply was short in the market during that period owing to price rise by 50%. Eventually, the organisation suffered and the leader was left red-faced in front of the share-holders.

As seen in the above example of the confectionary, the units worked in silos and lacked coordination. A seamless information flow between the relevant units on a common platform showcasing supply, production and sales progress would have helped the relevant units to act or make course correction without delay.

The sales team could have immediately recast their sales mix, focusing efforts/resources on selling more chocolates than biscuits. Overall turnover target could have still been achieved with proper information flow and a sense of togetherness.

A deep sense of belonging between an employee and the organisation forms when the organisation communicates the broad organisation plans along with unit plans and also celebrates success stories together.

Above all, the employees need to associate their progress with the progress of the organisation.

According to [44]Dr MP Ganesh, friendship networks in the workplace is one of the least focussed areas in Human Resource Management because of their informal nature. On the other hand, these networks play a crucial role in the flow of tacit knowledge within the organisation and are also crucial in building trust and reciprocity amongst employees, which, in the long run, lead to workplace synergies.

Such cross-functional networks would not only improve the workplace dynamics but also improve efficiencies and output. This sharing of information and ideas may lead to innovations too.

For an organisation, success is more than just hitting targets. Doing things the right way is a much healthier path in building an organisation.

[45]Simon Sinek believes that organisations should recognise teams that display an infinite mindset.

As per Simon Sinek, if the organisation rewards teams which somehow hit the target, despite not having ideal internal team dynamics and not teams that narrowly miss the target, despite having ideal internal team dynamics, it is sending a subtle yet powerful message to the rest of the employees that the journey is not important while only the final outcome is crucial, which is hitting targets.

Apart from not being able to sustain themselves in such an environment while being in teams not having ideal internal team dynamics, the members would eventually look for alternate workplaces. Such toxic teams would not be able to sustain themselves in the long run and in fact destroy the harmony in the organisation.

For employees to adopt the required values and right behaviours, the following could be done by leaders:

- Examples, both good and bad, must be showcased.
- Links between the right kind of behaviours and jobs must be created so that the right person is in the right job.
- Influencers and seekers must be identified within teams and must be placed for optimum distribution and influence.

While achieving targets is important and the teams that achieve must be duly rewarded, it is very critical for recognising the right values and healthy behaviours, as these behaviours and cohesiveness create a valued organisation in the longer run. This reinforces the need for defining the right competencies and behaviours as well as assessment of the two.

There is a difference between rewards and recognition. Reward is generally understood as more tangible and material, while an individual can feel recognised without receiving a reward since it is more intangible. Employing a good mix of the two would work wonders.

It is human psychology to expect recognition and rewards following an ably carried out performance. But, an atmosphere of valuing quality must be created, and the leadership must recognise the ones striving for excellence. The best side-effect of such pursuit for excellence is that it is contagious, and those employees that have the streak of striving for excellence will immediately take notice of this and try to be on the path themselves.

[46] *"People work for money but go the extra mile for recognition, praise and rewards."*

– Dale Carnegie

When teams are put on a recognition platform, the team members start working cohesively. They would hold each other accountable and would counsel each other in difficult times so that the team's progress is not hindered;

they would trust and help one another to succeed and try to extract the best outcome together.

Through this process, the team would benefit with some invaluable learnings – they learn that trusting and sharing is the foundation for success leading to good internal team dynamics. This could happen between two or more teams as well when they start working towards common goals. The synergies between them and the information flow improve, and eventually, they start working as a large group. This happens organically when encouraged by leadership, and it is highly beneficial for an organisation when a large number of people succeed in groups.

KEY POINTS COVERED IN THIS CHAPTER

- Induction and introduction of the best self-image
- Recognising right behaviours
- Involving operations units while building strategy
- Empowering teams to explore
- Synergies between cross-functional teams

KEY TAKE-AWAYS

ACTION PLANS

_____

_____

_____

_____

_____

_____

_____

_____

_____

_____

_____

_____

_____

_____

Epilogue

I am glad you read this book and hope there were some takeaways that will help you and your teams!

These aspects of people management have to be more pronounced in times of crisis like a pandemic such as COVID-19, an economic downturn or a natural disaster. Times such as these really test the organisation, employees and you—the leader or supervisor.

Your resilience and spirit will lead your team through trying times. The improvement in team effort and ownership will be clearly visible when able leaders showcase that intent, action and innovation are crucial.

One such leader, Anand Mahindra, during the initial stages of the pandemic not only spoke about employee safety but inspired others through commendable initiatives. He announced that Mahindra Group will get its manufacturing units to make ventilators and also offered to convert Mahindra resorts into temporary care facilities.

When leaders walk the talk, the trust and commitment that follow makes a lot of difference.

All the best!

Notes and References

1. https://en.wikipedia.org/wiki/Organizational_ culture, Jul'2020

2. https://www.treasurequotes.com/quotes/all-employees-have-an-innate-desire-to-contrib, Jag Randhawa, Jul'2020

3. Cable, D. M. (2019). Alive at work: the neuroscience of helping your people love what they do. Boston, MA: Harvard Business Review Press.

4. Glazer, R. (2019). ELEVATE: Push beyond your limits and unlock success in yourself and others. S.1.: SIMPLE TRUTHS LLC.

5. Edmondson, A. C. (2018). The Fearless Organization: Creating Psychological Safety in the Workplace for learning, Innovation and Growth. Hoboken, NJ: John Wiley & Sons

6. https://www.treasurequotes.com/quotes/ leadership-is-practiced-not-so-much-in-words-a, Harold S. Geneen

7. https://www.kennethmd.com/the-prep-framework-an-easy-way-to-give-excellent-impromptu-speeches/

8. Frei, F.X. & Morriss, A. (2020). Begin with Trust: Harvard Business Review. https://hbr.org/2020/05/begin-with-trust,

9. Lencioni, P., (2002). The Five Dysfunctions of a Team: A : A leadership fable. San Francisco: Jossey-Bass.

10. https://www.toolshero.com/leadership/lencioni-trust-pyramid/

11. https://www.slideshare.net/optimaltransformation/patrick-lencions-five-team-dysfunctions-48670463.

12. https://www.treasurequotes.com/quotes/as-we-look-ahead-into-the-next-century-leader, Bill Gates.

13. Dweck, C. S. (2008). Mindset: The New Psychology of Success. New York: Ballentine Books.

14. Tran, A. (2019). I am Not a Lost Cause — How I Fixed my Mindset. https://medium.com/mindsets/i-am-not-a-lost-cause-how-i-fixed-my-mindset-3cc7788cf629.

15. Lucas, B. (2016). https://theconversation.com/how-to-praise-your-child-why-simply-saying-well-done-is-not-helpful-66975

16. https://www.floridatechonline.com/blog/psychology/the-difference-between-transactional-and-transformational-leadership/

17. https://www.floridatechonline.com/blog/
     psychology/the-difference-between-transactional-
     and-transformational-leadership/

18. https://www.treasurequotes.com/quotes/it-is-
     not-the-strongest-of-the-species-that-su, Charles
     Darwin.

19. https://en.wikipedia.org/wiki/Kurt_Lewin

20. https://study.com/academy/lesson/lewins-3-stage-
     model-of-change-unfreezing-changing-refreezing.
     html, Kurt Lewin.

21. https://www.tata.com/about-us/tata-values-
     purpose; Ratan N Tata, 2006.

22. Ibarra, H. & Hunter, M. L. (2007). How Leaders
     Create and Use Networks: Harvard Business Review.
     https://hbr.org/2007/01/how-leaders-create-and-
     use-networks.

23. 24. Ibarra, H. & Hunter, M. L. (2007) How Leaders
     Create and Use Networks: Harvard Business Review.
     https://hbr.org/2007/01/how-leaders-create-and-
     use-networks.

24. https://www.treasurequotes.com/quotes/the-less-
     an-organization-has-to-do-to-produce, Peter F.
     Drucker.

25. Phillips, J. (2010). Three Innovation Strategies
     https://www.slideshare.net/jdpuva/three-
     innovation-strategies

26. https://www.treasurequotes.com/quotes/good-
     leaders-make-people-feel-that-theyre-at.,WarrenBennis

27. https://www.treasurequotes.com/quotes/what-gets-measured-gets-improved, Peter F Drucker

28. Dr MP Ganesh, Associate Professor, Liberal Arts at IIT Hyderabad

29. https://en.wikipedia.org/wiki/Behaviorally_anchored_rating_scales

30. Ibarra, H. (2015). Act Like a Leader, Think Like a Leader", Harvard Business Review Press.

31. https://www.treasurequotes.com/quotes/courage-is-the-power-of-the-mind-to-overcome-f, Martin Luther King Jr.

32. https://en.wikipedia.org/wiki/GROW_model

33. https://www.treasurequotes.com/quotes/a-boss-has-the-title-a-leader-has-the-people, Simon Sinek.

34. Goleman, D. (2000). Inspiration from Leadership That Gets Results, Harvard Business Review.

35. Pattanaik, D. (2013). The Author of "Business Sutra: A Very Indian Approach to Management.

36. Goleman, D. (1995) Emotional Intelligence

37. Willink, J. (2020). Leadership Strategy and Tactic. Willink, J & Babin, L., (2018) The Dichotomy of Leadership.

38. Oppong, T. (2018). How Expectation Shape Behaviour For Better or Worse https://medium.com/@alltopstartups/pygmalion-effect-how-expectation-shape-behaviour-for-better-or-worse-11e7e8fa7f4b.

39. https://en.wikipedia.org/wiki/Robert_Rosenthal_
    (psychologist)

40. Livingston, J.S. (2003). Pygmalion in Management.:
    Harvard Business Review. https://hbr.org/2003/01/
    pygmalion-in-management,

41. Pattanaik, D. (2013). Business Sutra: A Very Indian
    Approach to Management, New Delhi: Aleph Book
    Company.

42. Dweck, C.S. (2008). Mindset: The New Psychology
    of Success. New York: Ballentine Books.

43. Cable, D. M. (2019). Alive at work: the neuroscience
    of helping your people love what they do. Boston,
    MA: Harvard Business Review Press.

44. Dr MP Ganesh, Associate Professor, Liberal Arts at
    IIT Hyderabad

45. Sinek, S. (2019). The Infinite Game: Penguin.
    https://simonsinek.com/the-infinite-game

46. https://www.pinterest.com/pin/5666795
    65585329577/ -Dale Carnegie.